Into The The

# BACKLASH
PRESS

A pioneering publishing house dedicated to creating intelligent, vivid books. Established to inform, educate, entertain and provoke.

A Backlash Press Book

First published 2021
Reprinted 2024

backlashpress.com

Book designer: The Scrutineer, Rachael Adams.

Printed and bound by IngramSpark

ISBN: 978-1-9162666-4-3

All rights reserved. No part of this publication may be reproduced, stored in a retrieval system or transmitted in any form or by any means, electronic, mechanical, photocopying, recording or otherwise, without permission of the copyright holder.

Copyright © Robin Reagler
The moral rights of the author have been asserted.

Robin Reagler

**Into The The** Robin Reagler

*Backlash Poetry*

American Dangerous: Renée Olander
Bombing the Thinker: Darren C. Demaree
Clay Unbreakables: Natalia I Andrievskikh
Phantom Laundry: Michael Tyrell
Tattered Scrolls and Postulates: Joseph V Milford
The Life in the Sky Comes Down: Bruce Bromley
Unfinished Murder Ballads: Darren C. Demaree

*Backlash Journals*

#1
#2
#3: Provoke
#4
Isolation

For Carrie and Pearl

**Into The The** Robin Reagler

Cover: barn photograph by David Reagler

# Contents

Epigraph                                                              11

One

Damage                                                                15
What the Fortune Teller Said                                          17
Big Swim                                                              19
The First Evening, After the Great Leveling                           21
My Own Bible Story                                                    23
The Yellow Store                                                      25
Town I Know: A Mural                                                  27
Call It "Her Becoming"                                                29
Dream Manifesto                                                       31
Warning To Bridge Trolls, In At Least Five Voices                     33
The Drowners                                                          35

Two

Reach To/Ride To                                                      39
The Heights                                                           43
Message to the Goldfish                                               45
Western                                                               47
Everybody's Autoerotica                                               49
Charlie is Lucky                                                      51
Mobius Strip                                                          53
Sixteen Lines                                                         55
Our Strangers                                                         57
Hangnail                                                              59

## Three

| | |
|---|---|
| On the Big Screen | 63 |
| The Graffiti Artist | 65 |
| The Sky Wonders Out Loud | 67 |
| Nightly I Visit | 69 |
| The Hotel Sublime | 71 |
| Instead of Happiness | 73 |
| Call It "His Secret" | 75 |
| She Stepped on the Weather | 77 |
| Duke Nukem | 79 |
| Dreck | 81 |

## Four

| | |
|---|---|
| Green Selfie with Twombly | 85 |
| Crazy in the Head | 87 |
| Film Noir | 89 |
| Easy Chair | 91 |
| Into The The | 93 |
| Time = X, Mind = Y | 95 |
| The Age of Irony | 97 |
| Something Like A Spine | 99 |
| Acknowledgments | 103 |

Into The The
Robin Reagler

**Into The The** Robin Reagler

Where was it one first heard of the truth? The the.
*Wallace Stevens*

**Into The The** Robin Reagler

# One

**Into The The** Robin Reagler

# Damage

You could remember the house you were born in.
You could remember the red voice of the sea.
You could be hours driving down a freeway in someone else's car.
You could be crossing a desert in a Western no one's seen but you.
You could roll down the windows and let the sunshine kick your cheeks.
You could open your mouth real wide.
You could ask a silent question.

You might watch mirages lift off the asphalt like somebody's silly theory about time.
You might count the tumbleweeds, adding up the numbers in your head.
Your thoughts could float like ashes in the air.
You could memorize the rules or you could break them like knitting needles.
You could imagine your mother.
You could drive through a wall of smoke.

After miles of road and rolling plateau, you might reach a fading white adobe church.
You might get out of the car to stretch your legs a little.
Maybe you'd walk inside that place of worship, dip your finger into an urn of cold water, and make a bullet-shaped drop on your own forehead.
Maybe you'd sing a passionate song to the stained glass.
Maybe a woman would glide up behind you like a childhood memory of wind.
She might ask you if you lost your lamp.
She might make a prediction about weather.
You could tell her you know her.
You could read the messages zooming out of her eyes.
She might pound on your chest until the feathers flew out.
She might steal your name.

You might rush back to your car, feeling afraid, feeling changed.
You might examine your reflection in the rearview mirror and wonder why

the picture won't stay still.
You might spit in the dust before you start your car.
You might touch your body all over, making sure that it's still okay.

Pray.  Pray with me.

You could evolve.
You could seed the earth, a thousand paper cranes released along the highways
we call America.
You could drive through the sun.
You could write down your version of everything you've done.
You could lie.
You could love me.
You could turn the page.

# What the Fortune Teller Said

Most days the water comes in so still you can
Hardly tell that it's moving. From where you stand
You see a forklift humming down the dock
Doing something. You don't know what.
You walk through the aisles of grocery stores
Looking for treats, in case of company. Good
Sense pops off your skin like raindrops to the duck.
Life, friends…you try to say, but you get bored.

It's no great shakes to see into the future.
I'm three floors up; the alley's filled with shards
From crystal balls I hurl in haste, in anger,
At the unnamed thing I hate--that alley wall.
To throw things makes me see a little better.
I rub my eyes, call down to my next customer.

**Into The The** Robin Reagler

# Big Swim

If you feel around with your
fingers   there is a corner
to every sin     Upon finding
that tight spot   one must
remember what to do     Listen
   I have been out setting
this trap     Cabbage is cheap
    Nobody has seen me     If
I eat right   I'll grow big
gills   touch my tongue to the
ocean floor     Who were your
friends before this     Since
that film   I can't masturbate
and how does anyone know anything
   say their mother   for
instance   or garage doors
Things that go up   down   down

It is raining     Coach says run
    Humidity in this tiny room
smells tin     Coach gives his
boy a rub down     of the back
    More water moves   down
gutters   across the eyes     The
boy is losing all feeling     Now
he looks for his gloves     Now
my room   full   I think   of
books     Are there pictures
What sort of sounds     Who is
needing the *great* blow job
It is only summer     Someone
knows what this feels like    I
am thinking   someone knows what

**Into The The** Robin Reagler

this means   if it bleeds   I don't
have to shout     The autoerotic
parakeet   sings out

# The First Evening, After the Great Leveling

Now, now, now, and now,
it arrived in the form

of an arch
enemy toting a tome on

alchemy. I sewed up
its head with a needle

and thread, and it may
seem improbable to you, but clean

clothes fell
from the sky. A lullaby

spilled out of my mouth, as dew
dampened the ashes

we slept on.
Nobody was alive.

I woke up once
before dawn, watched the flames

reach into my eyes and wondered
whether my shadow

raised
or lowered the intrinsic

value of this wall.
A spiral

**Into The The** Robin Reagler

takes me down inside my body and then back
out into the night:

stars– spiders– flying eyeballs–
where I am

more angry than before,
a falling feeling, small new nation.

# My Own Bible Story

My wings got wet tonight for the first time
In a long time. What I say is true. And then
The cry–it leaping from my throat, I spy
A picture spilling holy lights all moving
Around. I close my eyes. They still be there
On a screen I see that really cannot be.
I know this. And I notice in the air
The creatures that keep looking back at me.
The limbs of trees from here look very pleasant.
I could go down there; that would change things though.
The branches I can love– I love them slant.
But that's the way the sky makes plans. Suppose
You're looking up the sky and you see passion.
I saw the wheel, but only for a second.

**Into The The** Robin Reagler

# The Yellow Store

Tonight the moon
is tiny, gold, just
enough to make it
moon and the bridge

which wants to take
us there begins
by the sycamore
tree.  Stars drop

from the moon's
closed eye down
to my little
brother who closes

both eyes also.
I sing from
your glowing porch,
Yellow Store.

What have you done
with the children
who made you?

Light stops
making sense.
The dreamer
is the dream.

Beacon, portal,
moment, star.

**Into The The** Robin Reagler

# Town I Know: A Mural

I want you to see it.

The blue archivist wallows, mild-mannered in the Sabbath sunset. Anyone can tell you: he's pining.

The healer, hands never in his pockets, strolls down the sidewalk past a wild field of sunflowers that pierces a former floor and sooty bricks. A mercantile building used to be there. The black and white linoleum tiles crack open and bake in the summer sun.

They all know my daddy, they all know my momma, but they're not sure which of the little rainbows I am.

The geezers on that sloping porch are trading stories about their wars.

Remember when the grain elevator became the tallest building in the town?

When the teacher looks right at me, I feel the needles in my mind.

My pal on roller blades, she moves like fluid down my street. Hello, she sings, slowing down slowly, looping around in the neighbor's driveway. She sits on my step to smoke a cigarette and chat.

The insects hop from limbs to branches, their legs singing cranky country songs. A lizard lets its back blend into bark. Green leaves feel good about themselves, but the fruit in this tree looks embarrassed.

A billboard reassures us that Jesus is loving us all.

The philanderer crouches down as though to tie his shoe. We know what he's thinking.

I want you to see it. A girl wearing gingham lights a candle that smells like

**Into The The** Robin Reagler

America.

I know some rainmakers who meet secretly in the wings of cathedrals and talk about time. But that happens over in Europe. We don't do those things.

In the town I know, we were a family: I was the brainy one. My sister was the socialite. My brother was the class clown.

Zooming back from Memphis, driving down the highway in his pajamas and red bathrobe, the blue archivist hurries home. When the State Trooper peers out from under the wide brim of his hat, it's Sunday morning. The speed limit broken up like clouds in the sky. The floor of his Lincoln Towncar, littered with not-recycled beer cans. What's your rush? asks the trooper. Late for church, explains the archivist.

The sixteen-year-olds laugh like savages. I flirt with them to cheer myself up.

The towheads spend the afternoon fishing, and the lake actually falls asleep for a few minutes. It happens every couple of years.

We are proud of our sunsets. I want you to see it. Perched in the western sky, the sun's rosy sleeve shimmers like an excellent idea.

That pretty lady--she hasn't been back in years--cut her hair, moved to the big city, makes big money, dances only with strangers.

The blue archivist, he remembers it all, and the truth is always bad news.

Darkness, I have been so lonely. Lie down with me in the grass and read me our future in the constellations of fireflies.

Now here's our friend Walt Whitman ambling down the road as the night coats our drippy lids and the fear spurts out a bit.

We name ourselves the age of something certain and dream the simple dreams of simple sleep.

# Call It "Her Becoming"

if a breath
then a storm
if a feeling
then, in a flurry of shame

she looks out the window
steals a singular meaning
and even the clouds clamp down over the small cottage

she shudders
feeling herself perhaps
inside the grasp of some immense, fur-lined hand or mouth
anger tapping at the edges
inside the confines of her human membrane
and everything dying
a girl
put away safely, in a diminishing
while
while air presses against her skin from all directions
while a thousand secrets
otherwise known as
selfhood
clamor like a rash
a rocking chair
the day wilting like a sack of cabbages
bought at the supermarket, left
in the back seat of the car
last summer

if alive
then in a realm of unnumbered time
if love
then blurting out, merging with

**Into The The** Robin Reagler

the old, retold stories

and she remembers her mother

# Dream Manifesto

One blink and then a thousand bats fly out of the notches.

Night slips black sequins under their wings.

Where I'm walking (a cavern of hell) fire grows on the trees like leaves.

You can taste it: the skin, bitter, the fruit, sweet.

Fire is the marriage of anger and shame.

That's when I sewed the secret list into a stranger's hems and cuffs.

Bats sound out in the labyrinth of your skull.

It seems like something you'll never forget.

But you will.

Moon pie    dragon fly    black eye    lullaby.

The children sing in slow motion on the school bus to the moon.

I stand where I've been standing for quite some time.

But I had understood betrayal all along: furtive like roots, furtive like hate.

It can turn sleep inside out.

**Into The The** Robin Reagler

# Warning To Bridge Trolls, In At Least Five Voices

I would seem fancy if I were grown up

Is it always this chilly

Do we *got* to wear shoes

Can you listen to the questions when I try hard to ask

How many faces

Have the dogs been fed

Would the blue dog wear shoes

Does the dog want to eat us

Would someone call her mother if a little girl got lost

What just stopped loving us

We are coming to a bridge

What just rolled off

It's just like a story Daddy told about goats

Keep your shoes on, Tom

The first song just rolled off

Should we run like dogs when we get to the bridge

What will you sing if the bridge is blue

**Into The The** Robin Reagler

What will you wear if I act my age

When the blue dog arrives, can I wear your scarf

Ain't them other kids chicken, look

If no one dies, will you be disappointed

Do you feel lonely when we all hold hands

What you sing will warm you up

Tom is not fancy but he doesn't care

How much longer 'til we go back to momma

Wouldn't you rather cross bridges on Tuesday

What lives in the space between girders and water

Tom, Tom, do *we* believe in the troll

Hello, grand central, could you send out some firemen

Tom, I'm scared-- promise not to tell

Fill up the space with the song about bridges

What you put in the space will push back on the riddle

# The Drowners

As the childlike bodies sink like sinkers down,
a song

escapes from their lungs. The air bubbles contain a long
ballad of how

these terrible terribles happen to happen
and why.

*Why, why*. That is the elegy sung for the drowners as pine
body-cartons

get covered with fistfuls of dirt and sensible stones.
Believe

that the stars stare down a kind of punishment from the sky, and we
are alone

by being above the water, breathing air. Despite the factual shore,
they

are closer to the world of details than they were the day
before.

For us, forgetting comes naturally. The new music in
season

bears witness: a strong feeling erases any lesson.
Listen.

**Into The The** Robin Reagler

# Two

**Into The The** Robin Reagler

# Reach To/Ride To

1."I like blue," says the little boy into
my ear and then I tell him this story:

>Where the gloss cameos the twirling stair,
>Where it twirls down into the dark, the glimmering
>Pond, the gloaming, and one large bullfrog
>Glances around bigly to the baby dragonfly--
>That's where the story begins, where I was born.
>
>Half an acre of darkness, the warm
>Breathing of songsters revving up the night,
>While their pale robes whisper in and out of shadows
>That arrange themselves quite out of sequence
>Along the brushy shore of the pond. And they all know
>To come here because of what their bodies tell them
>And they dream smarter than us and know nothing about love.
>
>The frog nods his head to the orchestra, then
>Across water to the baby dragonfly because he is
>Smiling and he is glad there is no mention of love
>Because this world is separated from a huge messiness
>(He has a feeling) and besides, it is his first birthday.
>The mom-birds are dealing with eggs and hunger.
>Day-sky cringes at the edge of the eyesight. Soon
>Morning will come and people and everything will
>Change but we can hold our breaths until some more
>Passage-time until the deepest voice of all calls
>From somewhere inside our ears saying, *Hey, time to go,
>This vision is shutting down*, and the stairs vanish.

"Zoom," says softly the little boy
Closing his eyes, "Zoom."

## Into The The  Robin Reagler

And the boy touches my hand and sits in my lap
Like it was made for him and he fits okay and then
He says something nice to me, something like. . .

And then I realize that there is no boy, that I have
Been (what would they say?) fabricating, making
This stuff up, lying through my teeth. And yet,
If there is no little boy,


2. What should poetry do?

When *I* ignite, I will do it
With flash, like a parked car,
Your car, that you parked for the afternoon
In its usual place with the meter full of change.
Cursèd disappearances! As soon,
The expected mirage, and then nothing,
Your head, slowly, down with the weight of this day
And the other ousters whispering to you *Now it is gone*
Because now it is gone.


3. And what would come next, you might ask
(For there is some courage to the way I let these stories roll
Off the table top, one after another, knowing that they are
Everything, knowing what I know about the table).

And what would come next might be scorpions, desert bugs, the smell
Like steel wool, a man turning the metal crank and the asker
Asking in that sly voice, that confidence,
*How are you/but really?*

Beside us now, a box of tools and the wiped hands
Down the green coveralls of the mechanic and snapping
The engine cover down, he says *This time this baby's
Gonna fly*, so the unlikely crew (present, for their presence
Is needed for the story to end) shifts up their eyes
Half-shocked by the blue sky which is not blue at all,
Really, and the engine sputters severely

While they all pause, knowing that the hero will leave soon
With his airplane good-as-new. But for now, for this brief
Moment he is stuck in his smallness, in the smallness of our eyes.

**Into The The** Robin Reagler

# The Heights

*Hoohooooooo*

a man kneels down
before an even
more powerful man

his hand imagines
a cat
with lonely fur

curtain        seltzer

weapon        lover

as the train whistle
scratches the face
of distances

a powerless man lives
with phrases
stuck in his head

*the barber's neck,*
*the barbarian's*
*necklace*

and weather frets
as it lights up
a pane of glass

## Into The The Robin Reagler

the insomnia blows bubbles
that steal
the breath away

inside a house
these incidents
unburn


kettle            wrestle

pressure         muscle


and a man kneels down with nothing
to say,
not a thought in his head


after the echo

after all the echoes

# Message to the Goldfish

Listen to me, fish.
You can feel pain underwater.
My ears were unhappy once,
But I was not up to making

Large demands. I am breaking
Into an evening. It is not sexual
Although that was one
Consideration. The rocking

Chair seemed enough for me
For the seeing--sun, sun,
The acrobatic air--I never
Leapt from my mind not once.

I try to remember the sound
I was born in. I try to remember
A bowl is not the sea. Why
Should we ignore the pain

In our ears? I am older.
The sun makes this sound too,
But only when the sky
Turns inside out     and turns.

**Into The The** Robin Reagler

# Western

A full moon always.  And cows.  Not
Being afraid of anything, I inquire:

What happens to good faith
When young cowboys fall over?

Where did the world of Passion/
Action run off to?

My life is not all television,
But Little Joe's not back yet

From church and every day our herds
Dwindle, getting themselves rustled

Out from under our worldly possessiveness.
Pa looks thoughtful as usual.  He must be

Considering widows.  I'm big as a horse:
Yes, yippee-ki-yi-yay, and boy can

Hop Sing cook up a mess of stew
After our sinister chores are checked

Off the list.  Here at the Ponderosa we stay
Busy.  Words like *swagger* and *wrangle* work

Almost always.  Sit still, you'll get ambushed.
I'm much happier in the saddle, cursing

Up a storm, singing a ballad about blood.

**Into The The** Robin Reagler

# Everybody's Autoerotica

Somebody's Shoes

      Notice a peony just about into a kind of electric endeavor with a beaver hat worn atop the skull of a fire hydrant; they recite the rotten hypothesis quietly indenting the left side of the sky. Ding! I feather up the swiftness of a long spine of color. Pictures keep yellowing me out of my coat. Hurry! Sick people darken the insects like sidewalks.

A Test in French

      After the quickly bridges tugging at my earlobe like a crime at the edge of an auction swam up to the surface of a prayer book, I felt like a somber, somber ninny not fooling anyone in public. With bon jour certainty of the bingo winner, you have been had. Glamorous prizes itch--why did you scratch lazily over the surface to see what you unlikely raked in scarlet weather?

Kissing Cousins

      While nouns are sweating and frog-gigging, clams squeal midnight up the downy foglike yodel. If flying notes lick the balmy arrows, then lilting coughs and blood pies will follow your animal grandmother to her stone. An opera requires safety flowers with AA batteries, not included. Cast away your parsimony riddle while your backyard tool shed still has a chance.

Bridges

      Awful dominoes smell falling, mercenary of the totally ear of my funky yesteryear. Let's go with the fluttering can't-touch-this of the bossy mother selling the kids at auction like gone. The sad-tune (mother) flits spoons in the faces of insects singing, pretty medicine, pretty medicine, in the careless wind unzipping the eyelash dream inside the underwritten flash card of the night.


Rear View Mirror

      "Monkey see, donkey blue," as they say in Mesopotamia. A gator waded out crossways in the ancient bad luck of April phosphorescence. With skull holiness, the actors eyeballed themselves evolving waferlike in the bending mallow. Boys gorged on question marks beneath staring lights. Every sitting princess furiously raining down on my pup tent will meddle with prosperity. Egypt, go home, I dare you.


A Willow Tree

      Agonized over crystal whiz, the two birdies wailed lost cities as pretty in catalogues. The painted plains rumble like brides (quack, quack) and I mean industrial haste! Come along, follow me, Dad. So that a chowder knows quality as Jack-in-the-box instant epiphany. Sentencing out of a mild tourniquet. No crisis, pal. Just whistling.

# Charlie is Lucky

Those of you in mountains without a dreambook
feel the ominous sequins in your eyes and are lost

A wish is feathery like
a too friendly pocket

The changing is changing
a bad landscape erupts in a pale halo

He has a failsafe plan against darkness
but has written it with footprints in the snow

*Ping!* The map unwraps itself
time seizes the dream of us

Ask a question

We? we are part of what
Is what and real and doing wheelies in the sky

A frozen web collapses
Coaxing white into the season that dares us

**Into The The** Robin Reagler

# Mobius Strip

That bean in your eye surprised
me, as they say in the comics.

I had been slaving away in my pseudo-
detective agency all day long, but due to doom
psychology was always feeling
either jaded or beatific.

Then you came along,
so handsome in your distress.
Like a phony sunrise.
Like an airplane crosses the sky.
I said I'd do what I could.

But the answer (in time it appears)
had nothing to do with the black bird, or us,

whose life is not big enough.

**Into The The** Robin Reagler

# Sixteen Lines

There were five or six mirrors in all.

Worse than that, there were fish swimming.

Not fish but some small white shimmers of the eye.

My eyes are not gray; they are incomprehensible.

I am speaking from a room you know well.

Spaces exist and it's a real problem.

Every now and then, I see a clock.

And a dream gets challenged, like everything else.

Things that are flung, things connected by string.

And it all started with my eyes.

There may be a formula for expression that I don't know.

How sad, the little light-up goldfish (blew out).

I feel forced to tell you to pay attention.

Some days the doctor comes, takes a mirror for himself.

Until I am finished, I am not-finish (with eyes).

Just one at a time, O they are not the same, the walnuts.

**Into The The** Robin Reagler

# Our Strangers

The elders construct no wings but say that they will fly.
A scratched sidewalk drives around the city. Clouds

Wilt. A skyscraper sprouts arms out of anger. An
Intruder yawns and retraces steps, perhaps his own.

So it is now that you confront the new now. You are
That place, a somewhere, an empty smell.

Mechanically—yes—you glance out at the music,
The cubes of air rocking the rose-colored atmosphere.

And black and sky and black sky are worth nothing. Your
Denial is not answerable. We are feathers.

**Into The The** Robin Reagler

# Hangnail

12:17 A.M. I subject my toenails to a little

stopgap analysis. Conclusions reached?

On earth you matter. Sure

the circumstances change

but you're with us or you're against us.

I have my own little aphorism:

On earth the circumstances alter.

One day it will go like this:

A penniless boy will arrive very late.

If you have the question, you have the question.

Go ahead, take my place.

Step into the garden.

**Into The The** Robin Reagler

# Three

**Into The The** Robin Reagler

# On the Big Screen

An announcer says they
are "back at the ranch,"
that the story will
continue. They have
made us this promise.

There is no story
after death. Stated
with authority, there
is definitely
no story.

You lean against the wall of a dark cave only the dark
is blue instead of black, not as cold as I had expected,
still, I shall say, chilly. Sinking back into the wall
a little, you breathe easy once again, feel better, good
enough to look at the string in your hand and then up,
eyeing the white balloon hanging there above your head.

I think how it will rise soon, way above us, with its
slow helium. You think, *white face*. And see, in your
hand, the gray string that we are watching, fist
and string. Isn't it funny how no one will admit it,
that we want to see the grip go out, completely wound
down because that's death and that's what we came to see.

And you're comfortable with all of this, aren't you?

If, before death, there's
no plot, no hero, at
least it's in color,
and we can watch it on
a big screen in bars.

**Into The The** Robin Reagler

Take this minute:
that we are, hand
and string, "Come
on now, cowboy, any
old dream-come-true."

# The Graffiti Artist

Inventions germinate in his head.  He, NextGuy,
the astronaut hero of some dim underworld.

Let me in.

NextGuy has only the two-fisted for friends.
He wouldn't give me the time of day.

I worship him.

His spray-paints torch the color of tear gas.
A fire escape looms with an obese question.

I am under his spell.

The last cop tinkers around
Outside the corner store.

Will He notice me
With eyes of stars?

Like hell I bet--
Now, Next.

**Into The The** Robin Reagler

# The Sky Wonders Out Loud

I remember what I
                dreamed last night.
You were all there.
                In a flooded field
some poets waded in
                water up to their knees,
and they kept
                talking about angels.
It kinda made me sick.
                My friend the sun
wore a patch over
                one eye and seemed to be
in trouble. Three
                blue crop-dusters looped
around. I just wasn't
                ready, and I knew it.
The airplanes exhaled
                their science-breath
leaving codes across
                my side, and the poets,
certain in their ability
                to read these signs,
stared at the great mystery
                which happened
to be me. I tried
                to speak, but all that escaped
my mouth
                was tremulous thunder.
Then I woke up.

Nesting in my ear
                the same old bird

**Into The The** Robin Reagler

coos with the confidence

                of the new moon's suitor.

Satellites dangle down

                like diamond earrings blinking

at the future.


                Way down below I spy

a noisy little chicken

                I've seen before

just hanging out

                waiting for me to fall.

I try to be careful.

                The best place for failure

could be anywhere.

                The bird in my ear

sings extravagant sadness.

                The sun closes

an eye.  It doesn't help

                to worry.

# Nightly I Visit

the handcuffing stranger whose
mouth moves slow.  As he creeps
across the face of the blind
water I begin to remember
stealing jewelized vessels
from the exploiters' homes—
Fear followed by fear-not.
From my divided madness,
I am allowed to mail
six postcards a year.  I count
these syllables I send to you
so lost out there, so lost
in here, and I measure
what's left.  It's time to rest.

**Into The The** Robin Reagler

# The Hotel Sublime

*I am the lobby*
*You are the parrot in the cage*

The man named Amanda
gallantly opens the door
for the boa lady. The boa
she wears today snags
the eye--red, gold, jungle
green, and turquoise.
Her father made the boa
out of fallen feathers, so
much did he love birds.

The desk clerk notices the two
of them and pretends not to.
The man named Amanda 's
rent is three months in arrears.
The Hotel Sublime pipes in sea
breeze, a kind of Zoloft (TM)
for the gloomy lobby air,
but the couple finds no fault
with the drab environment.
They float in the newness of love.

*I am the elevator*
*You are the hat lady, singing*

Step inside. I will take you
wherever you wish to go.

**Into The The** Robin Reagler

# Instead of Happiness

A file folder     has noise trapped inside it
it sounds like a nail     getting pounded by a hammer
by a craftsman of limited skill and excessive emotion
The noise has an echo     it's a kind of bread     inside the iron
That cannot be eaten
a fear     that has its hidden hinges
in plain view but without risk of getting stolen
a turnip     not quite real
but abruptly     aware of my own     fear
I don't know when     I first fell     in love with your
adorable radio show     but every Sunday
as dawn begins to spur     a certain joy     similar to
the pleasure of counting     by nines     when you are not really
present     and yet     there     in just the way
that you meant to be

**Into The The** Robin Reagler

# Call It "His Secret"

His secret burns

His secret grows no his secret climbs

Up a telephone pole thinking

A better view better air

But no, so


His secret has something to say

It is surrounded by barbed wire saying keep out

It has lost its edges

And creeps across the air

He can smell it like he smells the future

Foam on the crests of waves

The ocean sends its garbage home, as he remembers


It is canceling him out


Don't touch it

## Into The The Robin Reagler

Don't lick it

(It would be like licking a loaded gun)

Don't even look at it

Hanging huge on the wall

Of a small house constructed of curses and sadness


Don't breathe so hard

In this house

Its stained walls

Raw ceiling

Scratched air

Its cautious roof

Managing these images

Controlling our eyeballs

Bigger than we are

Forever

# She Stepped on the Weather

Shut up, lawyers.

I stand on the palm of my hand, crying.

Spelling is my bird.

We dropped a groan so the laugh aspirated.

Ears joked, as if a coin could, over and over, commit suicide.

I behold violet lightning.

Beauty in the custody of a famous actor.

Now we can say it:

A bloom darkens, as earth unfolds.

**Into The The** Robin Reagler

# Duke Nukem

One the anger
two the gaze

three I got a
bit o' gun

zero sanction
burn my words

finger itch
loving thumb

wish me luck
for time gone dry

I gotta—

**Into The The** Robin Reagler

# Dreck

More often than not, I
dig it. The the.

Take yesterday. I
bought me a kasha knish, made
a wish, and stared at trash, an escape hatch. I visualized an intricate system of
spiky seeds carried by

                breath across and down, across, down. The dark seeds
harpooning and lodging into a gooey wall. Tendrils prodding their way free,
careening, curtseying, gulping
                down acrid air. The image = technicolor cartoonicity.
Then distraction slapped me upside the head.

Ope. I was home.

                Fifth floor walk-up. My knees
knew better. The surface surfed beneath my feet. I watched. I

felt watched.

**Into The The** Robin Reagler

# Four

**Into The The** Robin Reagler

# Green Selfie with Twombly

Night swimming in the hot springs

domed by the stars, the stars.

Underwater noise purposefully burbles

in the forest pool. Since 1962

the ears have heard the roar.

Whistle and the weather follows suit.

The leaves float, the leaves sink.

I am a fish.

**Into The The** Robin Reagler

# Crazy in the Head

Everyone suffers.
I, for instance, long for the Goodyear blimp.
So empty is my sky!
Listen: the birds sound nervous.
I squeeze my eyes shut to convey another psychic message warning the President:
        BE (I rake my brain hoping for a perfect word) CAREFUL.
Last night my boots disappeared while I slept on my own front porch.
Some days the doorbell rings, and I'm scared. I decide to start smoking and then
change my mind. Somehow I just don't feel safe for democracy.

I amble up to the Question Box
and write an amorous note
to my darling. The message is not quite true,
but I know it will make her happy.

Then I call up some expert I barely know
and have a pointless argument about a billboard I saw while I was driving
        around on the Loop. "Is it an airplane
or a metal hand waving at space?" I hear myself asking.
Simultaneously I stare at the blue blades of an oscillating fan, which leaves me feeling dizzy.
The voice repeats "two-handed engine" too many times.
For some reason I secretly record the discussion on tape and mail it to a private detective
        in the capitol.

Either the dog talks, or the ice cream truck changes its tune.
Either the incumbents forget to listen or we are the innocent victims of the ranting
        alto sax.
Either the pineapple people protest, or a cow licks the mechanic's face for salt.

## Into The The  Robin Reagler

Either everyone is talking or no one is listening.
Either the sexy girl (as I remember her, not as she really is) or the boy wearing
the leather bomber jacket from your dreamy days in Soho.
Either the wet knife or the gasping wound.

I stay angry
but not because no one
is listening to me.

Given space for reflection, we learn what little we can.
Believe me, I heard an authoritative voice narrating:

*A new trend was edging up on us.*
*We were a part of it and yet it would make our decisions for us.*
*We dozed like iron sculpture in the booming sun.*

# Film Noir

Ransom note said
*meet you at midnight
under the neon
windmill.* Now

        the brown sky sags.
        Leaves hang from wet trees
        like little trench coats--
        He's in big trouble.

An ashtray:
smoke seeps from a cigarette
trying to escape,

        and everyone's got an alibi but him.

The girl—she
always knows
what to say,
and telling lies gets easier, the more you practice.

        Will he come to love
        the beauty of three words
        said in a single breath?

The Law
guns the engine and waits for him
in his dreams

        until screaming night-cars chase him
        into wide-awake.
        His hope is for a narrow escape.

**Into The The** Robin Reagler

And you,
you are the Dream of Law,
desiring what you desire most,
a spectator to spectacular play.

*It must change.*

# Easy Chair

Like sandpaper the

at breathing.  Dust

birdsong.  Listen

the rhythm.  There

Under the surface

are wrestling for

and gold lets blue

as uncles purse their lips.

an announcement

up to the level

of history are shouting

flames kick at

dawn likes to linger.

syllables are working

flags into electric

then counsel

is no hurrying this.

of summer, rhymes

the early lounging hours,

fly skyward

An infant makes

that raises old stones

of eyebrows.  The pages

out the changes, as

the furnace walls where

Your windowsill's burning.

**Into The The** Robin Reagler

# Into The The

Next fade of habitat into
Wide that shrill octave
Cast a tidal eye
At sweetie


This dump =
One lost
Above-dungeon stumbled-down
Fill-in-the-blank


*Jazz as if a nerve*

                *of never-never*

*wasted and fevered*

*in a stack of maze*

                *like experimental gas*

*and forever roarable.*


A roaring praise

                tests my fingernails, the

riverbank's

rivery burial is

## Into The The Robin Reagler

                    *its handkerchief, its*

*phrase bleeding*

*inside a woman....*

A breeze trap  
Scrap of sloth  
Topple from air  
Let them

Signed, the OUTLOZ

# Time = X, Mind = Y

I can't sleep a baby

cries somewhere the kitten curious squeezes
into a narrow
invisible
slot

      of the apartment I hear the

fish go *ping* in its bowl and a wasp bangs
gingerly against
the window

           a stealthy feeling stalks

me through daydreams until I am
scared and
then I am
      okay

        The clock
           does my thinking
for me

when it asks, *how is it that I got this
moment*
      *at your ear*


Consciousness is a layer

        of dust on the wing of an
airplane

**Into The The** Robin Reagler


and so
when the present moment opens

       into a new moment, that's
when I remember


Amelia Earhart

and the dream of becoming birdlike

and then
                            I imagine her

flight over
            the flat desert floor

across a blasted ceiling of blue

and fire

and blue

# The Age of Irony

Here in a morning of silver birds and silver dollars
the acrobats snicker,
the orphans lick their fists,
a majorette glides down the newly paved asphalt.
I have a funny feeling about this video.

The mothers blaze at the appointed hour.
God calls the wanderer on the pay phone.
"Hello?" resounds the helpless voice inside the booth.
The connection is poor, as usual.

It is morning. A double agent
places his ear on the outside of the glass, hears half the conversation,
and writes some numbers in his secret book.
I know they must be numbers.
He's tapping his foot.

On the altar
the baby monkeys play a little game.
They outline pictures of things they know on their mother's back--
hyacinth, fire ant, giant raindrop—
And she tries to guess.
Silver birds sigh in the alcoves.
She is ready for a new game, frankly.
I can tell by the way she doodles
lines in the dust.
Her pictures echo the thoughts of the booming sun
and an edgy fear of the changing seasons.

The Imitator asks me to share a cab ride to the airport.
I'm unsure of the question, unsure of the feeling.

(My mind races,

**Into The The** Robin Reagler

always a step ahead,
telling me what to say.
I am the usher,
taking good care of you,
helping you through this thing.)

On the outskirts of this idea
cats are wearing the sacred ponchos
to keep themselves safe from the sneering rain.
The video camera whirs away.
Someone slams down the telephone receiver.
Another recording.
The monkey family trudges in a bundle home.

How can we trust what our eyeballs are telling us?
We don't understand, but we aren't really trying.
We are anticipating paychecks and wondering where to cash them.

You stay right here,
silent as your childhood chemistry set,
faithful as the apostles. I've got to blow my nose

which runs gently like time
seeping
out of the ears
of time.

So long.

# Something Like A Spine

The graveyard sanctioned everything I meant
to furnish with the ripped color of azaleas, nosing
spring into the burnt air smell the trolley brings.

Walking colored the ground as pattern, it was so soft.

Believe that I arrive at this point, wedging myself in.

We leave the trolley far behind, so it is just us
and tombs and tombs and azaleas.

The burnt air smells.

The graveyard sanctions all these tombs, which
are placed on top the ground like checkers
since New Orleans is one big marsh and can't
keep even a coffin decent in its belly.

In terms of geography, the mind is expansive, a huge
tank-- certain people would say garden --bounded by
sanctions imposed by pretty much everyone, it seems.
The rules aren't quite clear, but I know they're against me.

The graveyard lets us walk it through.

## Into The The  Robin Reagler

Sometimes a frost, but we cannot feel it.  It is
mostly warm here.  No one knows where to make
a mental record of the deviations.


The mind makes no comment on the places outside the self.
It used to.  Then came--adulthood, I will call it.
I do not try to rearrange in my mind the tombs and flowers,
the azaleas.


(But the world is accessible.)


New Orleans gives their dead more credit, you know,
not just stones to mark the spot but tombs, like Egypt,
a privacy of a suite, a luxury vehicle, practically.


There are rules about sentence structure, rules about
what to say.


My throat says it has just swallowed a seed.  I know that
this is a lie, a fucking lie.


The ground, soft, the tombs, on top.


It's just we haven't seen each other in ages and so what
if I just fall in love with you all over again.


The birds, everything I hear comes from them.  They
sit in the azalea bushes not pretending to be flowers,
but pretending to be what the birds meant.

(I did not know what the birds meant.)


Tombs, bushes, birds, the ground, soft, the smell, refusing
to rest for anything.


The world is accessible.


Desire is distance. This, the graveyard will allow us.


Regions occur either within or without the mind. The mind
does not realize the difference. If I could only insert,
here, my rejection of one or the other, the within or
the without, the region or the mind. But that is not allowed.


Desire lay siege to the all-of-us, colored the floor of walking,
so we left open our bodies, we just kept doing it.

# Notes

The title of this book refers to the last line of *The Man on the Dump* by Wallace Stevens.

The characters in *Western* come from the TV series *Bonanza*.

*Everybody's Autoerotica* is inspired by Gertrude Stein's *Tender Buttons*.

*The Hotel Sublime* is written with fond memories of the Hotel Chelsea.

*Duke Nukem* refers to a shooter video game released in 1991.

*Green Selfie with Twombly* references the painter Cy Twombly and the so-called green room at the *Menil Collection*.

In *Crazy in the Head*, the phrase *two-handed engine* comes from *Lycidas* by John Milton.

*It must change*, the line from *Film Noir*, comes from *Notes Toward a Supreme Fiction* by Wallace Stevens.

# Acknowledgments

I'd like to thank these loved ones for their support: Sheila Black, Marcia Chamberlain, Lucy Chambers, Ruth Dickey, Laura Mullen, and (in memory) David and Joanne Reagler.

Several of these poems—*Damage, Everybody's Autoerotica, Call It Her Becoming,* and *Something Like a Spine*—appear in *Dear Red Airplane*, a chapbook published by Seven Kitchens Press, published in 2012 and re-issued in 2018 as part of the ReBound Series.

The following poems have also appeared in these journals:

88
ACM (Another Chicago Magazine)
American Letters & Commentary

Americas Review
Bayou Review
Colorado Review
Cutbank
Delmar 2
Denver Quarterly
EOAGH
Five Fingers Review

Iowa Journal of Literary Studies
Iowa Review
Maverick Magazine
Mayday Magazine
Mississippi Review

North American Review

Easy Chair
On the Big Screen
Mobius Strip
Town I Know: A Mural
Crazy in the Head
Everybody's Autoerotica
Call It Her Becoming
Time = X, Mind = Y
My Own Bible Story
Reach To/Ride To
Into The The
The First Evening, After the Great Leveling
Sixteen Lines
Western
The Yellow Store
Film Noir
The Heights
The Age of Irony
Message to the Goldfish
Warning to Bridge Trolls, in at Least Five Voices

**Into The The** Robin Reagler

Pavement
Pleiades
Ploughshares
Portland Review
Southern Poetry Review
The Weight of Addition (Mutablis Press)
The West Review
Zocalo Public Square

Something Like a Spine
Dream Manifesto
Big Swim
Charlie Is Lucky
The Drowners
Damage
Our Strangers
Hotel Sublime

www.ingramcontent.com/pod-product-compliance
Lightning Source LLC
Chambersburg PA
CBHW021146060526
44107CB00146B/1329/J